# The Essential Introduction to Experience Management

Published by TSO (The Stationery Office), part of Williams Lea, and available from:

**Online**
**www.tsoshop.co.uk**

**Mail, Telephone & E-mail**
TSO
PO Box 29, Norwich, NR3 1GN
Telephone orders/General enquiries: 0333 202 5070
E-mail: customer.services@tso.co.uk
Textphone: 0333 202 5077

First edition 2024

ISBN 9780117094659

SD000159

# Contents

# Foreword

The year 2007 was very significant. It was the year that the transition from the service economy to the experience economy began in earnest. The experience economy had been extensively predicted and described by Joe Pine and Jim Gilmore in their milestone book *The Experience Economy* in 1999. Their thesis was, 'The experience economy is an economy in which many goods or services are sold by emphasizing the effect they can have on people's lives[1].'

The launch of the iPhone in 2007 and, more importantly, the software development kit for the App Store in 2008 enabled individuals to own every process they consumed via their smartphone. Pine and Gilmore's predictions became social facts. Through mobile applications, individuals became co-creators of their experience in every sector. They became the trusted source of information for their friends and families. Now we have a generation of experience influencers who are often seen as guides to how we (should) live. As high-speed internet became abundant a power shift occurred, putting consumers in the driving seat. The business had to contend with massive disruption. Winning with a great product or service was not enough; it had to create and support a great experience as well.

The experience economy was about to replace the dominant service economy, which had engulfed the industrial economy in 1987. Each economy requires frameworks, measurements, tooling, roles, and concepts. A crop rotation specialist had no place in the industrial economy, and the time and motion analyst died out in the service economy. How would transitioning from the service economy to the experience economy play out?

I asked myself what would become of frameworks which provided the best practices for the service economy – concepts such as service level agreements, configuration management, change management, and service desks. Soon after the concepts, the service management tooling followed. It started with rudimentary standalone products such as IBM's Info/Man or BMC's Remedy. It evolved into the sprawling integrated systems that now dominate the market, such as ServiceNow. Could the same systems and tooling that supported the service economy become a stumbling block for the experience economy?

As a technology leader in innovative industries, I wondered whether these service management frameworks could adapt and survive the transition. My 'aha' moments came in 2008 at the world's largest bank. We were in the middle of the aftermath of the financial services meltdown. I observed two things at the same time:

- The net promoter score (NPS) I had so vehemently supported since Fred Reichold introduced it to us at HP in 2003 was perhaps not the predictor of behaviour I had expected. The bank recorded a negative NPS score of -47. Yet neither employees nor clients left the bank. That left me asking, 'What is the right level of investment in NPS?', and is analysing experience not more complex than a simple number derived from a survey?

- We were rebidding a unified communications contract (voice, video, personal and team messaging, voicemail and content sharing). During the preparations, we found that each supplier (in good faith) was reporting solid green dashboards. Yet the business leaders in the bank were

---

1    Pine, B.J. and Gilmore, J.H. (2011) *The Experience Economy*. Boston: Harvard Business School

complaining stridently that the service was a disaster. It was then that I learned about 'watermelon metrics'; green performance on the outside, concealing red sentiment on the inside.

I concluded that we needed change and to focus on experience-level management that went well beyond service-level management. Assisted by Marco Gianotten of Giarte, we introduced a new concept that we would later call XLAs. The core idea is simple: understand the sentiment and then work in partnership between suppliers and businesses to do what matters for the audience.

Nobel prize winner Max Planck said: 'When you change the way you look at things, the things you look at change'. I have found this to be true of every innovative venture I have ever engaged with. Indeed, it is a prerequisite for innovation.

My crucial discovery moment was a brilliant thesis on experience management by Marcel Broumels, written in 2007. Marcel invented the term XLA when he initially targeted the building facilities management market[2]. His thinking was clearly appropriate for every situation where service was transitioning to experience.

Through Marcel, I discovered a whole new world of pioneers and developers, all dedicated to understanding, leading, guiding and managing the experience economy. In 2020, a group of like-minded service management veterans came together: Neil Keating, Lisa Schwartz, Bill Barrett, Ken Wilson and me. Our purpose was to understand and tame the experience beast so we could help organizations survive and thrive in the experience economy.

We helped launch the XLA journey of early adopters such as global digital employee experience companies and educational and social institutions. We created a vibrant worldwide community.

Today, as Experience Collab, we have extensive experience designing and implementing XLAs around the world. We have codified our experience in certified education and training and are globally licensed in multiple languages. This publication embodies our learning and today's best practices. In our volatile, uncertain, complex, and ambiguous world it is the start and not the end of your experience management journey. There will be many iterations over time.

I am sure that this publication will help everyone in every maturity phase to start and continue their experience expedition confidently and enthusiastically.

Alan Nance, 2024

---

2     Broumels, M. (2015) Research, Experience level agreement. Available at: https://marcelbroumels.wixsite.com/experience/research

# 1   What is experience?

When was the last time something happened to you that affected how you felt? Yesterday? Today? Five minutes ago? The odds are it was recent. What you went through was an experience. An experience is something that happens and makes us feel a certain way, and we encounter them all the time. It can take a short or extensive amount of time, but it always arises as the culmination of various moments that we collate into one memory.

Experience is universal and happens to us in all the various roles we play throughout our lives. For example, a customer will have a particular experience with an organization, as will an employee. These are the two roles that Experience Collab focuses on when it comes to analysing experience. As we will see, experience has become a crucial factor in customers' and employees' relationships with organizations.

Looking at definitions of experience within this setting, positive/negative customer satisfaction, interactions, and occurrences throughout them, are all moments over time that equal an overall experience for an employee or customer. If we want to understand what an experience means in a business sense, it's essentially about customer satisfaction or dissatisfaction about you, your brand, your product or service, all built up by their interactions over time. When someone is asked how they feel, they weigh up all the interactions they have had with you and come to what is, in their perceptive reality, a balanced conclusion. People will do this consciously or subconsciously. Recent events may have more of an impact in that moment, but experience will always be valued and concluded on when looking back over time.

## 1.1   Facts and feelings

*'Feelings are facts. Emotion is a fact. Human experience is a fact.'*

**Eleanor Roosevelt**

Feelings are both the cause and driver of experience. An experience will make us feel a certain way and that will drive our feelings towards it in the future. If you receive a positive experience from a restaurant (for example, customer service that not only knew of your dietary requirements from your booking but also recommended particular items) you're likely to feel content and secure about that experience. The restaurant has shown that, from your perspective, you are important to them. This will increase the chances of you visiting again. An essential part of experience, noted here, is perspective. Perspective shapes experience; our experience of something is our perceptive reality of that thing. How we feel about an experience becomes our reality and ends up becoming the key detail relayed to friends and peers. If feelings are caused by experience, then it stands to reason they should be measured to ensure the right experience is being given. Say an organization, as standard, provided employees with new laptops and access to specific applications but didn't ask:

- What do they need?
- When do they need it?
- What devices do they need it on?

If we don't consider these questions, we risk creating the kind of experience where the entity providing it becomes something that the person resents. They may feel that they, their role and personal circumstances have not been considered. An employee from our example above may be working at different sites and prefer to work from a device like a tablet. Someone working in design may be given applications that the organization assumes are useful but is missing one important to the role. This will cause, at best, mixed feelings from the start that can only worsen with time if unaddressed. If you prolong this the feelings that people hold towards the product or service, and by extension, the organization, become fact for them; facts that easily become aspects to warn others of.

The feelings that influence our attitude towards various entities aren't formed from just one interaction. Humans tend to give second chances; they are built up over the many interactions that form an experience. While experience can comprise one moment, most of what we would call experiences are constructed throughout various moments over time. If our feelings towards something remain negative continuously, it lowers the chances of our ever wanting to spend time with it again. It will certainly influence our future attitudes if we encounter it or something similar. The optimum way to make the consequences of negative feelings towards something less likely to occur is to measure these feelings and work with them. How we do this is expanded upon later. For now, let's explore further the fact that experience is built over various moments over time.

## 1.2  Moments over time

When we interact with an organization, it is rarely with just one component. Even an experience that comprises a few moments, such as visiting a café, involves interacting with various components that build the experience. The barista provides customer service and the customer interacts with the technology provider when they pay for their product. When the customer is sat down, they indirectly interact with the part of the business that sets out requirements for interior design and décor as they take in the atmosphere. All of these interconnected components of the organization come together to provide an overall experience for the person. Throughout each of these interactions is the chance for experience to ebb and flow. Someone may have a positive and helpful interaction with the barista before having a negative one with a slow payment system. When experience drops, people often encounter something we call experience anxiety. This is the uncertainty and stress that come from a poor interaction in the makeup of our experience. If and when this is resolved the person will then encounter experience relief; the feeling that comes from understanding that the experience is about to improve again. Understanding the different components throughout an experience is important, especially for organizations that want to improve the experience of their employees. They need to understand the various services and interactions an employee has if they are to be better enabled to identify the problem areas.

# 2 Why does experience matter?

If an experience is made of multiple interactions, or transactions, organizations tend to focus on a single transaction as a moment of truth and experience. In essence, they often take a snapshot view. However, as we know, this is not the experience in full. A snapshot is just one part; if one is taken as the whole measure, it can lead to false positives as the other moments over time are left out. If we buy a car from a garage, our experience likely starts off good due to the excitement of the purchase. We may then find its fuel consumption isn't great, causing our experience to drop, but the suspension is smooth, and the features make journeys stress-free; so our experience goes back up. Say then we encounter a fault. Our experience goes down; however, we take it back to the garage to be fixed. It is usually after this fix that we as a customer would receive a customer satisfaction (CSAT) survey to gather our sentiment about the fix. Because the fix has been made after some time with the fault (a good example of experience relief after experience anxiety) we will probably provide good feedback. However, what happens at this point is the garage assumes our positive feedback to represent our overall time with the car, and so it comes as a surprise when we express a mixed experience and indecision whether to continue our custom in the future. This is because one transaction has been used to define our experience when there have been many moments over time culminating in our final experience sentiment.

As humans, we are programmed to focus on the negative aspects of experience after the fact, even if the overall experience was neutral. Remember, the definition of experience in a business sense is the culmination of interactions with your product/service. After many of these interactions a sense of experience anticipation (the kind of experience we come to expect) is built. These may not be experiences with your organization's products or services, but anticipation being formed from the experience with another. It's unfortunate, but we're much more likely to inform our friends and peers of a negative experience than a positive one. Biologically speaking this is because our amygdala, the flight or fight response apparatus of the brain, has remained largely unchanged since the days of early humans living in hunter-gatherer societies. In the modern world, the danger is no longer the wolves stalking us through the plains but a negative experience. If we have a poor experience with a company, brand or service our amygdala kicks in and encourages us to warn others of the 'dangers' of said experience: for example, 'Don't buy this brand!' or 'Don't trust this company for x service!' This shows how experience can cause us to influence others, and why it is so important. In a world where customers and employees have more power than before and can share their experience with thousands of people researching reviews, and where goods and services are no longer the be all and end all, it is crucial to consider experience and experience anticipation. Experience shapes our opinions of products and services, and alters our actions and decisions accordingly. We may decide to reject the services provided or walk away from the organization itself.

When good experience is provided, the results are amazing. Organizations with good employee and customer experience are more profitable than those without, with much of the reasoning surmisable from the above. Good employee experience encourages productivity and engagement, with engaged organizations outperforming unengaged ones by 21% according to Gallup[3]. On the other hand, a poor experience, as well as impacting organizational productivity, can encourage an employee to leave their role. Frustrating or anxiety-inducing experiences at work may be seen to be

---

3    https://news.gallup.com/businessjournal/163130/employee-engagement-drives-growth.aspx

caused by poor management or a perceived lack of support/good culture; all common causes why people leave their roles. In the past employees would think of their pay and continue in a company; however, in our current world where the motivating factor for the up-and-coming workforce is no longer just money, it is clear that experience is important. Employees aren't willing to overlook their personal growth or wellbeing for the sake of their pay. If they're consistently receiving what they perceive as a poor experience in their workplace, they'll leave and look for more meaningful experiences elsewhere. This highlights the importance of perspective mentioned in section 1.1. The employee's perspective on reality is their reality, so organizations should identify what is important to them and work to implement it to improve a key factor in their decision to stay with or leave an employer.

# 2.1  What about my organization?

Experience is not important just to the employee and customer; the organization also benefits from improving it. Six key benefits of experience management for organizations include improved employee happiness, improved employee productivity, increased customer loyalty, stronger employee retention, increased profitability, and competitive advantage. We will look at each of these in turn.

## 2.1.1  Improved employee happiness

If an organization can transform the employees' experiences and resolve their concerns about their products or services they will feel supported and listened to; not to mention happier that potential stressful experiences with work-related products and services are less of a hindrance. When our concerns are heard and resolved we feel positive and supported. If organizations can prove to employees that they will support them with the concerns affecting their ability to work, and understand what they need and want to work, this will help to create a more content workforce.

## 2.1.2  Improved employee productivity

Happy employees mean more productive employees. A University of Oxford Saïd Business School team found, from a group of 1,800 call centre employees, that happier employees were more productive and made 13% more sales than those reporting less happiness[4]. The employees achieving more were not staying at work late either, but using their time more productively, their mood predisposing them to do more with what they had.

Looking at the other side, a term that often equates to low productivity is 'unengaged'. Employees who feel unengaged translate to the global economy missing out on $8.8 trillion, according to a 2023 Gallup report [5]. For many organizations engagement, and thereby productivity, ends up being a target rather than the norm. However, this target can be more easily reached by providing a good experience for employees and keeping them happy and content at work, enabling and encouraging them to perform as productively as possible.

---

4    https://www.ox.ac.uk/news/2019-10-24-happy-workers-are-13-more-productive
5    https://www.gallup.com/workplace/393497/world-trillion-workplace-problem.aspx

### 2.1.3  Increased customer loyalty

From a customer perspective providing good, personalized experiences increases customer loyalty. By providing an experience geared towards what customers appreciate and find important from their interactions with the organization, you craft a personalized experience that puts them at the centre of the organization's attention, at least for their interactions and from their perspective reality. Their interactions with the organization then go beyond just a service and become something worthy of their time. The value of time is an important concept in the experience economy. If a customer does not see spending their time with your organization as valuable, they will look for others to provide this. It is thought to be five to seven times harder to gain new customers than it is to retain current ones. Encourage that retention by identifying what is important and providing aligned experiences.

### 2.1.4  Stronger employee retention

When employees are content and able to be productive, they are less likely to go elsewhere. This works with the regularly reported factor that wellbeing and a sense of purpose rank alongside, if not higher, than money as the main motivating factor for the modern workforce. If an organization is seen to be supporting its employees through positive experiences where they are valued and enabled to work as productively as possible, they are more likely to stay. Anything too far removed from this and the money they are earning will not prevent them from looking elsewhere.

### 2.1.5  Increased profitability

As mentioned in section 2.1.2, increased employee productivity leads to increased sales. In general, engaged, productive employees can produce more. A study by Ohio State University found that just a 1% increase in productivity leads to 1% increase in shareholder value, with regard to a raw production environment[6]. In an office environment it's clear that more tasks being completed will equate to more billable services being completed, and thus, increased profitability for the organization. Enable better productivity by providing a better experience for employees.

### 2.1.6  Competitive advantage

Often seen as a result of the advantages above, organizations that manage experience, that are seeing the resulting increased employee productivity and contentment, have a competitive advantage regarding their culture. They strive to create an environment that employees want to work and spend time in, which can continue to generate the organizational rewards that XLAs bring, such as increased profitability.

---

6    https://luxafor.com/the-link-between-productivity-and-business-profitability/

# 3 How to measure experience

If we know experience is cumulative, it raises the question of how something continuous, and in continual change, be measured. There are many ways of gathering sentiment, from interviews to special meetings, and even regularly mining social media and sites such as Glassdoor for sentiment towards your organization. However, since the last method encourages a more reactive approach and interviews and meetings are resource-heavy, We find the most common way of gathering sentiment is via a survey. These are regularly distributed sentiment surveys to find out what people (employees or customers) feel about the products and services they use most often. Organizations identify which areas of these products and services are most important to employees, and ask questions surrounding these that aim to gather the all-important feelings towards them.

## 3.1  What about CSATs and other surveys we use?

Your organization probably already measures some form of customer or employee sentiment. However, this tends to be in the form of surveys that, though good at providing a sense of experience at one moment in time or the context to investigate experience, do not, and are not designed to, measure sentiment. Let's look at two common types of survey that organizations use: customer satisfaction surveys (CSATs) and net promoter scores (NPS).

### 3.1.1  Customer satisfaction surveys

CSATs are good at obtaining sentiment for one moment in time, but they do not ask about experience. They are designed to measure a single transaction within those many moments that comprise an experience. In addition, the transaction that triggers a CSAT survey for a customer or employee is usually at a point where a potentially negative moment of experience is occurring; for example, after an IT support ticket has been closed or after a fix has been made on a car. This can lead to biased results where the organization receives data influenced by experience relief, whereas in actuality the person is mostly having a negative experience. This leads to a disconnect between positive feedback at one point, followed by negative, and the potential consequences that come with it. Because they measure just one point, CSATs cannot measure experience as a whole. Lastly, CSATs do not provide a true representation of the organization as only those who have, for example, logged a ticket or encountered an issue receive a CSAT. Because an average of 50% of issues go unreported, CSATs do not represent the sentiment, or satisfaction, of the whole organization.

### 3.1.2  Net promoter scores

NPS surveys are found in many industries and for good reason. These can be useful as they measure a form of experience, typically by asking a customer how they felt about an overall interaction or experience with an organization. For example, payment card machines can ask about overall customer happiness after a customer interaction has taken place in a shop or café. However, because they ask just one general question, there is no context to the data provided. Organizations can end up knowing people are unhappy, but they don't know why. To fully measure experience, the most important aspects of the experience need to be identified and measured so that plans can be made to improve the experience going forward for the customer/employee.

# 3.2 Measure periodically

Instead of measuring sentiment on a transactional basis, organizations should gather it regularly. This is to prevent sentiment surveys encountering the pitfalls of others. Sentiment surveys should be conducted without a preceding trigger event. Experience Collab recommends measuring sentiment monthly. By doing this, organizations will regularly be generating experience data to tell them how people feel about their products and services, enabling them to regularly identify the problem areas in experience and address, often before they become a serious problem.

So how does an organization start measuring experience? Not only are there steps to the process; organizations will also want to know how it connects to them and their business goals. To assist in visualizing the process and guiding organizations, Experience Collab has designed the Experience Management Framework (EMF) and Experience Optimization Framework (EOF). These are two interlinking processes that illustrate the connection between experience management and the organization as well as providing an iterative process with which to continually manage experience.

# 4 Experience Management Framework

The EMF is Experience Collab's overarching framework on experience management. It is an overview of how experience can be managed within a business context, as shown in Figure 1. Starting with the link determined between the experience wanted by employees or customers and the business outcomes of the organization, the framework goes on to illustrate the ambitions that organizations will draft from the overall experience wanted. The ambitions will form individual experience-level agreements with which the overall experience can be measured. Beneath the ambitions, the framework takes into account all the factors that enable accurate experience measurement, known as experience indicators. Lastly, the framework displays the overall experience score, being created via the XLAs, that will go on to impact the experience outcome and ambitions. New ones will be created or current ones retired as experience is being measured.

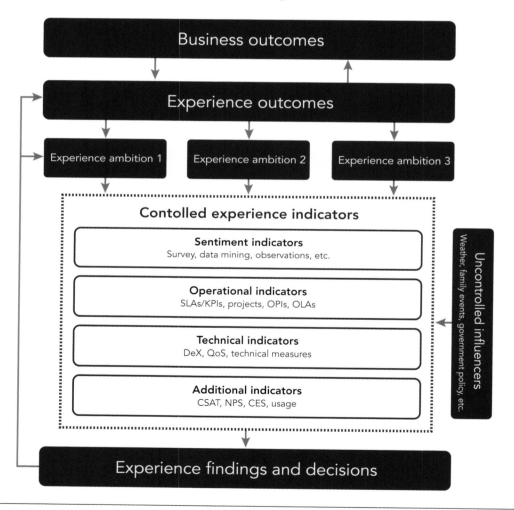

Figure 1  The Experience Management Framework

# 4.1  Business outcomes

Starting with the overarching rationale behind any experience management initiative, every business operates with some kind of outcome in mind. Be it financial or otherwise, a business outcome is a noticeable and defined result from work conducted.

# 4.2 Experience outcomes

Moving down a level but staying with a similar message, the nature of experience management means an organization will have some kind of improvement or outcome in the experience it is providing to customers or employees. This is what an experience outcome is; a defined result in the experience of the people an organization plans to target with XLAs.

# 4.3 Experience ambitions

An experience ambition is the statement of intent for the kind of experience that the organization wishes to stage. You will note the ambition is linked to the business outcome. Experience ambitions should have an effect on our business outcomes. In a less altruistic sense, a better experience for your employees and/or customers can lead to better profitability for your business. Therefore, it makes sense that while the employee/customer experience is the focus, the wider effect on the business will affect the possibility and longevity of having experience ambitions in place.

If we have an overall experience ambition, we can break these down into individual ambition statements, as shown in Figure 1. This is where outcome words of the overarching ambition are extracted to create ambition statements that effectively focus on one particular component of the experience stated for improvement. It is these individual experience ambitions that form the basis of an XLA.

# 4.4 Controlled experience indicators

Controlled experience indicators are the various data points used to measure experience for the ambition statement/s they are assigned to. They are deemed controllable because of the influence that organizations can have over them. Broadly these indicators include:

- SLAs and KPIs
- Technical tool metrics
- Sentiment data from customers/employees.

Results from the above are controllable because the organization has power to improve the intricate components of them and thus the experience derived.

## 4.5 Uncontrolled influencers

As the name suggests, uncontrolled influencers are factors outside of our control that can affect experience. Rather than being something that can be improved or resolved, these are factors that need to be considered when building a fully contextual picture of experience. These include factors affecting the collective, such as the weather or political events, to factors that affect each individual person, such as family events, illness, or news from a friend. Employers cannot influence how these factors affect their employees; only work with them or understand them in relation to experience management.

## 4.6 Experience scores

Each XLA will have an experience score. This is a calculation made by aggregating the controlled experience indicators and it numerically represents experience for that particular XLA. In the case of multiple XLAs, it is also possible to take the average of all XLAs to produce an overall experience score for the stated outcome in order to give a general score of experience. However, with individual scores for XLAs, organizations can see where experience is thriving and where improvements need to be made.

# 5 Data types

The controlled experience indicators (XIs) are the primary data points that generate a score of experience for an XLA. Of these XIs, Experience Collab have identified three key data types:

- **Sentiment (X) data** The most important of the data types, X data represents the data being retrieved from sentiment surveys in response to what the XLA is measuring. While an XLA can omit the following two data types and still generate a picture of experience, it must measure sentiment. Without sentiment, experience professionals cannot obtain an idea of how people feel, and thus will be unsure on the problem areas to address.

- **Operational (O) data** This represents the results from SLAs and KPIs, the operational metrics by which we measure the product/service affecting experience. O data metrics include aspects such as response time to logged issues on phones or live chats, resolution time for incidents and availability of services. Alongside T data, O data acts as the context behind X data. Organizations must understand how people feel and why they feel that way; O data metrics can provide this.

- **Technical (T) data** This represents the metric results from any technical tool the organization is using to monitor the health of its devices and/or infrastructure. Through technical tools, organizations may measure device crashes, uptime and launch time for apps. Like O data, T data can act as a great context provider behind X data.

# 6 XLA types/maturity

As well as the different data types, there are various types of XLA. Four common ones include:

- Internal IT XLA to employees
- Outsourcing company XLAs to its customers' employees
- Internal companies to their outsourcers (and vice versa)
- Project XLAs.

## 6.1 Internal IT XLA to employees

Of all XLA types, probably the most common are internal XLAs that organizations, typically in an IT environment, design for their own employees. Logically this popularity makes sense. Measuring experience relies on being able to ask people for sentiment. Internal departments have access to employees and can readily ask about factors such as what's missing in their working experience and what they might want. Additionally, an organization has a clear idea of its business objectives and can therefore combine this and the easy access of sentiment from its own people and tailor an XLA to fit them both. When an organization designs its own XLAs, there is easier access to determining employee wants and needs, the experience now and to tailor ambitions to both employees and business outcomes.

## 6.2 Outsourcing company XLAs to its customers' employees

A slightly more complicated view comes in when considering outsourcing XLAs. This is a situation where a service provider has designed XLAs as part of their contract. This can give the provider an advantage over others who may not have XLAs; however, those from providers being applied to their customers' employees tend to be more generic. The provider does not often have direct access to its customers' employees, making the wants, needs, and determining the experience now more challenging to understand/determine.

Adhering to customer wants and needs also means the provider must tailor its XLA offerings, something it may be apprehensive about doing for all its customers since this could mean a variety of services provided to a variety of customers, potentially stretching the resources of the provider. What this means is that whilst the experience now can still be determined and passed onto the provider, the provider will look at its services and design outcomes based on those. For example, if the provider offers service desk support, it will look for the experience outcomes it can fulfil in relation to that. XLAs outsourced from providers to customers' employees will look the same but be designed differently.

# 6.3 Internal companies' XLAs to their outsourcers (and vice versa)

A parallel to the provider-designed XLA, an internal XLA designed by a company for its provider aims to answer the question, how does the company feel about working with the outsourcers? A very sentiment-driven XLA, this is one that a company will design itself, effectively following the usual steps of an internal XLA that is then put forward to the provider in an attempt to integrate experience management into the contract held between the customer and its provider. They can also be used as an additional measure above other XLAs/any operational and technical measures to make renewal decisions with the provider as well as work to promote good working relationships. Working to ensure good working relationships with dialogues regarding possible experience improvement can be a useful way of gauging whether the customer would want to stay with this provider.

# 6.4 Project XLAs

A project XLA refers to using experience for the governance of organizational projects. Projects often measure aspects from the service economy, such as time, cost and an internal view of quality. By incorporating experience management into a project, organizations can measure additional success factors, typically ones that employees are concerned about. These include questions like:

- Did we achieve the business outcome?

- Are employees now having a better experience because of the project?

- How was the experience while we were doing the project?

As well as deciding on the most appropriate type of XLA for your situation, the subject of XLA maturity also needs to be discussed. Excluding not having XLAs (effectively level 0.0), there are three levels of XLA maturity:

- **XLA 1.0: Sentiment only** Where only sentiment is measured. No operational, technical or other indicators are taken into account to contextualize why people may feel the way they do.

- **XLA 2.0: Multi data stream** Sentiment and other controlled indicators are taken into account when managing experience.

- **XLA 3.0: Persona groups** This is XLA 2.0 but spread across different departments/entities, thus ensuring that a more personalized experience can be created for the various persona groups within an organization.

We will now examine each of these in turn.

## XLA 1.0: Sentiment only

A sentiment-only XLA will ask questions about the 'what' of experience, but not the 'why'. In this case, an organization may design its own survey, having worked to determine its experience landscape and experience now, and decide upon experience improvement actions exclusively from the answers, or X data, they generate.

An organization may decide on XLA 1.0 as the level for its first XLA. It may be because of the lack of exposure to the subject or the subject's relative modernity and lack of mass exposure in the wider world that an organization may not feel comfortable trying to implement the whole picture. XLA 1.0 can also be suitable for organizations whose resources may not be as strong, either in physical resources, or where current employee responsibilities are stretched. The people power may not be there yet to provide a full contextual picture of experience due to conflicting priorities. Experience Collab recommends that organizations start with the next maturity level to get the most out of an XLA, but just measuring sentiment is a valid entry point.

## XLA 2.0: Multi data stream

XLA level 2.0 means incorporating other experience indicators as well as the crucial sentiment into an XLA. Here, an organization may also analyse O and T data to understand its experience landscape and associate relevant O and T data points to the ambitions that it sets out. This means it is better positioned to understand the context, the 'why', behind what people are expressing in the X data being generated. Because this is the XLA that can provide a contextual picture of experience, it is Experience Collab's gold standard for organizations starting out with experience management. As they get better and better at the art of experience management, and adapt to the science of it, it may be possible to advance to the final maturity level.

## XLA 3.0: Persona groups

XLA maturity level 3.0 is the same setup as XLA 2.0, but with multiple XLAs distributed across different persona groups. This means that the workload is increased from XLA 1.0 but also that more personalized XLAs can be designed for groups/departments/entities within the organization that all have unique experiences; for example, HR, IT or finance.

# 7  The XLA Stack™

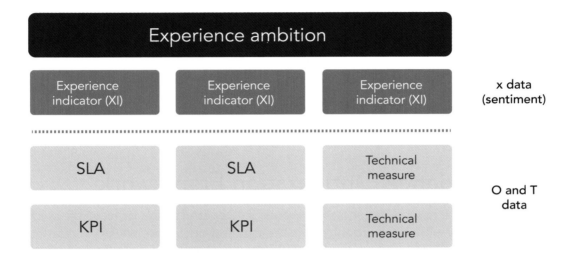

Figure 2  The XLA Stack

The XLA Stack, shown in Figure 2, is a visual representation of an XLA, essentially taking the experience ambition from the EMF and illustrating each with its relevant X, O and T data. Organizations that are managing experience with multiple XLAs will find it beneficial to study the XLA Stack model as it provides a variety of messages. As a template, it is the blueprint with which to note the ambitions and associated data points currently in operation or due to be. It can then become a quick view of an XLA that is easy to understand for people who aren't familiar with experience management. Lastly, it visualizes the relationship between sentiment and the other supporting experience indicators. The X data tells us what people feel. If organizations can then link supporting Xs to sentiment, they know which data points to look for in order to identify the possible context behind sentiment and where experience improvements need to take place.

# 8 The experience journey

Experience management is a journey. While the destination of experience improvement is of course where we want to be, the journey is equally important, for experience management is an iterative journey. XLAs are not a one-and-done initiative; once plans and actions have been made to improve experience, the organization should retake the journey to revise the experience management and adjust it in accordance with the continually evolving employee/customer experience. To visualize the iterative nature of experience management and guide organizations not just to their destination but back to start the journey anew, we have developed the Experience Optimization Framework (EOF).

## 8.1 The Experience Optimization Framework

The EOF is a six-stage framework, as shown in Figure 3. It illustrates the process by which we grow awareness of experience within our organization. We can find out where we are in relation to it, and where we want to be, before determining the kind of strategies we can take to enable our journey there and implement XLAs. The EOF then provides best practices and guidelines on embracing and ensuring that experience management continues.

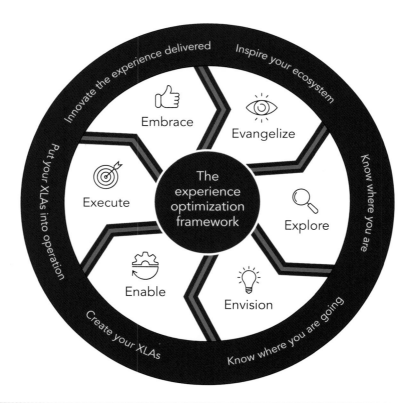

Figure 3  The Experience Optimization Framework

The circular design of the EOF shows the iterative nature of experience management; experience is continuous and subject to change. Therefore, multiple iterations of the EOF will be required if we are to manage experience regularly and seriously. Not all experience concerns may be resolved after a couple of iterations; some may become apparent and the basis for a new XLA.

The EOF comprises the following six phases: Evangelize, Explore, Envision, Enable, Execute, and Embrace.

## Phase 1 Evangelize

Inspire your ecosystem. Before we can ask where we are with experience, we need to know if there is awareness of it within our organization. Do people know what it is, why it is important and what it means for fulfilling business outcomes and driving positive results? If not, an awareness of experience needs to be cultivated, specifically within the experience ecosystem, the sum of interconnecting and interacting parts that is our workplace. Organizations should spread the awareness of experience throughout the ecosystem as there is a direct correlation between the success of an experience project and the breadth of the ecosystem supporting it. They should understand the experience consumers, influencers, and try to engage with experience champions. These are people who are aware of experience concerns and willing to share them with the organization, essentially providing valuable insights into what people are finding positive and negative in their employee experience.

Everyone in the workplace has an experience every day and experience affects everyone. Organizations need to build a consensus of what they need to do and how they might do it. As the first stage of the EOF, Evangelize highlights the need for an organization to be aware of experience. Experience cannot be delivered by one person alone. There needs to be awareness of experience within the experience ecosystem to ensure support for an experience management initiative. Show people what experience is, why it is so important, understand how experience is formed and anticipated, and build momentum for the project.

## Phase 2 Explore

Know where you are. Now that experience is known and hopefully deriving excitement about where it could lead, organizations need to ask where we are now with regard to experience? It's good to have an idea of where we want experience to be, but we also need to know where we are in terms of our ability to carry out experience management and to understand the kind of experience our employees and customers want. Explore is centred around getting organizations in place and determining where they are now so that they can move forward effectively. A key component of this is understanding the current experience landscape.

### Experience landscape – assessments, discovery and experience now

Before we begin to measure experience, we need to understand the rationale behind it. There are many aspects to consider, such as current resources, skills, tools and budgets. Understanding these will make for a more efficient program and possibly a quicker return on investment. Generate a sense of vision as you move through Explore – what risks do you hope to reduce and what benefits do you hope to gain? What kind of experience do you strive for within the service, product or general organization?

To assist in determining the experience landscape, organizations will need to undertake assessments. Through assessments they can determine, often quantifiably, where they are today. There are generally four aspects of assessments to analyse: readiness, capability, experience technology, and the current experience now sentiment.

## Readiness

There are many things to consider when determining an organization's current readiness to start an experience management project. For example:

- **Culture** Is the company culture accepting of change? If the organization is not communicative or open to becoming more experience focused, an experience management project risks breaking down.

- **Leadership support** You may see the benefits of an experience project, but the all-important decision makers need to be on board as well. It is useful here to ask if they are also aware of experience management, interested or educated in it?

- **ITSM maturity** Of any current ITSM processes, what is the current maturity level? As guidance, an organization on a par with CMMI® model level 3 – under control is a fair indicator that it is mature enough to take on experience management.

## Capability

There are four key areas to consider when it comes to understanding how well-equipped an organization is to deliver an experience management project:

- **Process** What existing processes are currently in place, for example, when a ticket is logged with IT? Linked to the current maturity level of the organization, seeing the processes that ensure that level takes place provides a good indication that the maturity level is strong enough to see a project through.

- **People and skills** Do the people identified as taking on an experience project have the right or appropriate skills? Depending on their role within an experience project, the various team members may need to know information and concepts from different levels of the courses.

- **Technology** What technology is the organization using that may assist in measuring experience? Tools that assist in service management, enable the creation of surveys, or monitor technical end point health can all be useful technology to note regarding an organization's capability to measure experience.

- **Resources** Is there the budget for an experience project or the willingness to provide a budget? Investments may also need to be made, possibly in technology that better enables the measurement of experience at a later point.

  Linked to the above point, are there current, identified experience indicators that the organization is aware of? Does the organization currently measure SLA and KPI performance (O data), device health (T data) or collect some form of sentiment from its employees/customers (X data) in the form of CSAT surveys, NPS or employee reviews?

## Experience technology

Technology is a required resource for experience management. A typical XLA, implemented in an IT environment, will involve:

- **A sentiment gathering tool**  This can be a tool dedicated to building surveys, retrieving and comprehending data, but other options also exist.

- **An ITSM tool**  Likely to be already in use, this is where an organization monitors its SLA and KPI performance, making it the crucial means of gathering O data.

- **A DeX tool or technical tools**  A digital employee experience (DeX) tool brings together and analyses device metrics that lead to positive or negative experience; for example, app startup times or crashes.

- **A dashboarding tool**  This is where the X, O and T data from the past three points come together. A dedicated dashboarding tool, designed to build and understand dashboards and datasets can be purchased; however, Microsoft Excel or Power BI is also a perfectly acceptable way of representing the data we will collate to understand experience. Your organization may already have access to it with a Microsoft 365 subscription.

## Experience now

As mentioned, while it is possible to have an XLA without O or T data, it must measure sentiment. Before you can find out where your organization wants to go, you need know how people feel currently. Understanding sentiment in the current moment is called 'experience now'. By understanding current sentiment, an organization can identify the wants and needs of employees/customers so that experience can be improved for the future. There are many ways to gather sentiment and build a picture of experience now. For example:

- **Team meetings**  Asking people in a meeting is a good way of getting to know people's experience concerns.

- **Service reviews** With regard to an outsourcer working with an organization, asking the customer what has been working well in the contract is a good way of opening up the conversation to experience and where improvements could be made.

- **Social media analysis (e.g. Glassdoor)** Social media sites can provide an archive of sentiment from past as well as current employees, granting you possible access to current sentiment. While people tend to exaggerate online, social media offers the opportunity to write an articulated response that may not be as easy within a moment's notice.

- **Data mining (e.g. call centre collaboration tools)** Analysing recorded calls can provide good first-hand evidence of experience concerns being expressed; for example, from employees to a service desk or from customers to the organization. In this situation, the experience is fresh in the person's mind, meaning they may expand more upon their concerns here compared to if they were called into a meeting to discuss it many days later.

- **Exit interviews** Asking people why they have chosen to leave their job can provide insight into poor experiences as well as the good that stood out during the person's time. More importantly, people may be more honest in an exit interview as there are few perceived possible consequences at this time.

We find a survey tends to be the most common way of gathering sentiment. If you can gather sentiment from a series of recent CSAT surveys, spend time analysing and understanding all the comments. Each is a window into the person's perspective about experience. In this case, perception is key and the perspective reality of the person commenting is the reality for them. It is how they perceive what you are doing rather than what you think you are doing. Therefore, when analysing their comments, put yourself in their shoes and understand:

- Why have they said what they said?
- Why did they score the way they have?
- What were they thinking at the time and why?
- What might have happened to cause this feeling?

Understanding customer/employee perceptive reality is very important. A common question asked at Disney theme parks is, 'What time does the 3 o'clock parade start'? Many people would dismiss this question as the answer seems to be apparent. However, after analysing why people were asking this, Disney worked out that what people meant was, when is the parade, starting at 3 o'clock, passing by where they were. The people analysing these answers could understand the question from the customer perspective rather than their own.

In understanding the experience now, two key factors are to be determined:

- Wants
- Needs.

Suppose we want to improve the IT experience of our employees. Through experience now data, we need to understand what employees need from IT to enable them to do their job better, before understanding the additional factors that they'd want to support them. Note that you may not be able to give everything that your employees want; resources just might not stretch that far. However, you must provide what they need if experience is to improve.

Prioritize the identified needs, and link them back to the business outcomes. By doing this we ensure that we integrate the right outcomes into the experience ambitions that we will create soon. This ensures that each unique outcome we want to achieve will be the centre of an XLA.

Explore is the phase where you ask the important questions surrounding the commencement of an experience management project:

- What are the benefits? Do you want to increase productivity, engagement or innovation?
- What are the problem areas and subsequent risks of not addressing those areas?

## Phase 3 Envision

Know where you are going. Now that an organization understands where it starting from, it can make steps towards where it wants to go. Using the available data, experience ambitions can now be established for where an organization wants to be with regard to employee/customer experience while mapping this place to business outcomes. It would also consider economic values to map to XLAs and to understand the range of acceptable experience based on the resources available.

A key component of the Envision phase is the experience ambition. This is the statement of intent for the kind of experience to be staged. The ambition defines the economic values to be achieved, any dependencies to success, and contains quantifiable objectives.

When crafting an ambition, it is important to include ecosystem leadership, particularly the people who will be overseeing the XLA that this ambition becomes. In the EOF an ambition can have one of two definitions:

- **Intrinsic** Achieving the expectation that an individual has of an experience. This could be better enablement of their productivity or a positive, valuable interaction with a service desk.

- **Extrinsic** Achieving the business value assigned to an experience. This could be higher productivity, sales, or increased retention.

It is possible that one ambition can incorporate both definitions. For example, a good service desk experience may lead to better sentiment surrounding the service, but improved productivity is good not only for the employee but also for the organization's business outcome.

### Range of experiences

When creating ambition statements, and in experience management, there is a tendency to think only the best experience possible should be worked for. However, this does not need to be the case. Firstly, the resources may not be there to provide that experience. Secondly, people who are affected currently by what they see as a poor experience will likely be satisfied with one they feel to be good enough. Someone might want the best, top-of-the-range laptop to work on, but as long as they have one that enables their work and minimizes hindrances they will be content enough.

Likewise someone who has just run a marathon won't demand the freshest, most chilled water; they will accept some that is room temperature because of their needs in the moment. If an outstanding experience can't be obtained in the current state, one good enough for the circumstances will be welcome and nonetheless seen as an improvement in the perceptive reality. If we know sentiment for a particular service is negative, resolving those issues to bring it up to a good enough level will be a welcome change regardless.

### Mapping XLAs to economic benefits

As well as understanding the range of valid experiences, we should also work to understand the economic benefits of each XLA. Along with the above, this will help bring an idea of what is an acceptable improvement given the current resources as well as what that improvement could mean for the organization. Looking at the EMF, this links both to our business and experience outcomes. We want to improve experience, but by doing so, we also want to see the benefits take effect in our business. Therefore, it is helpful to map each XLA, by way of the experience ambition, to an economic benefit. For this purpose, as shown in Figure 4, Experience Collab identify five types of value: commercial, efficiency, productivity, customer and future.

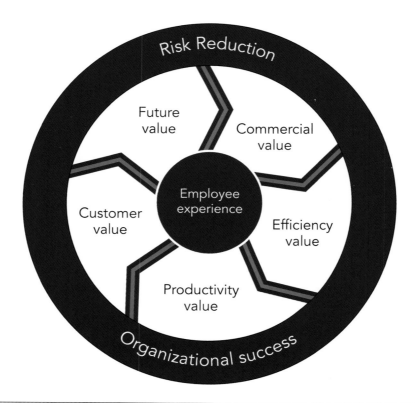

Figure 4  Five economic values of employee experience

## Commercial value

Centred around sales and brand, commercial value is concerned with how the XLA results in additional sales revenue/net profit for the organization or in stronger brand awareness. The choice between these two possible values can be determined by the needs of the organization. Sales is a very direct kind of value, very important to an internal organization, and something best suited for a commercial organization. Brand, on the other hand, is more indirect, important to an internal and external view, and suitable for all organizations.

An example of an XLA focused on sales would be to enable a sales team to work from wherever they are. One focused on brand may be to elevate the customer experience beyond what it currently is. This could be achieved directly by focusing an XLA on customers or indirectly by supporting employees to deliver a great customer experience. This not only raises the brand reputation but also works to encourage new customers and current customer loyalty, thereby providing commercial value.

## Efficiency value

Efficiency means providing the same output for less. This may include less time, money or other organizational resources. Prior to the experience economy, the service economy's main goal was to drive efficiency. Now in the experience economy this effort to efficiently carry out a service is only viable if the experience and value remain the same.

For example, an IT service desk can drive efficiency by taking staff attention away from admin tasks like changing passwords, by providing self-service or virtual assistants. However, while some will find this a suitable option and IT can say they're achieving the same with less, other people may still wish to speak to support staff regardless. The question here, that should be asked when mapping an XLA to the efficiency value, is whether the experience is just as good or is this a false efficiency value?

## Productivity value

Productivity differs from efficiency because it focuses on doing more with the same rather than the same with less. Most organizations have a productivity value, and it is a key theme for an XLA. When it comes to the experience they want to deliver, organizations usually ask the question, 'How can we enable our staff to work better?' Some examples of this include:

- **Onboarding** How can we ensure that new employees are enabled from day one?

- **Stable technology** How can we deliver minimal disruptions to the working day?

- **Enablement solutions** How can we understand the perceptions of our customers when working with our services, and how can I make this better?

- **Office environment** How can we ensure that employees are enabled to perform their role, working from anywhere?

## Customer value

As the name suggests, customer value is about how important/valuable your products/services are to customers. Mapping and then measuring this with an XLA is key to ensuring that customers perceive value in their interactions with the organization. When mapping customer value to an XLA, consider factors such as:

- Does the product/service meet customer expectations of what they need?

- Is the product/service available when the customer needs it?

- Do they find it worthy of their time?

Consider how you can understand customer value and design experiences that meet their expectations. Mapping an XLA to customer value works to encourage customer loyalty and has a direct impact on commercial value.

## Future value

Experience management is an iterative journey. Experience professionals need to focus on providing experiences that enable protection and improvement of the future value of a product/service. By mapping XLAs to future value, we may work to enable innovation, reduce future risks or win future customers.

Considering future value can also put the organization in a better position to fight the gravity of expectations that come with experience. Raising experience to a good level is an excellent initiative, but don't assume that everything will be good once that level is reached. Experience expectations from customers and/or employees will soon be at that level, meaning we need to innovate and improve upon what has been achieved to raise the experience level correspondingly.

## The experience economy

The mention of value is key to experience and XLAs. Value is a core concept of the experience economy, the aforementioned economic phase that businesses enter when they realize the value of experience being held by their customers and employees. In the experience economy people place a strong value on time. Customers have conflicting priorities and will choose where to spend their time. Therefore organizations who deliver experiences worthy of their time (that they value) are more likely to be chosen. If we don't do this customers may at best tolerate our services but not engage with the company, or just walk away.

Look at something like "quiet quitting", the workplace phenomenon where employees carry out the bare minimum within their job. Often, the cause of this is a sense that the organization isn't fulfilling something for them. Whether it be a sense of purpose or providing what the employee feels they need, choosing to quietly quit is a clear sign of disengagement. Employees need to be given a workplace experience that they want to spend their time with, not just something that pays them.

## Money value of time

One of the core concepts of the experience economy as it moved away from the service economy is how time has become a valuable commodity. People have realized the value of time, consciously or otherwise. One example, keeping to an IT theme, arises from the fact that just under 50% of IT issues aren't raised to the service desk[7]. People would rather deal with some IT issues themselves if the service desk is deemed too difficult or slow to contact. Many issues are ignored completely, affecting not only experience but also performance. If someone is delayed by several minutes a day due to minor IT issues they cannot be fully productive, in the same way that a stone in a shoe can add time to a walk.

However, organizations are realizing this. We see this in concepts similar to Apple 'genius bar' set-ups. Many IT support service desks now offer drop-in/pop-up support stops where the employee affected is working, making it a simple task to find support in the way that they want. We do need to understand, however, the difference in attitudes towards the money value of time between customers and employees. The amount of value that an employee generates is directly proportional to the value they perceive from their time spent. In other words, they need a return on the effort they put in. For customers, experience professionals need to recognize that the amount of money customers willingly pay, for any experience, is directly proportional to the value they perceive from the time they spend. This all leads to a key point made by Pine and Gilmour in *The Experience Economy*: you should design experiences that make your customers and employees want to spend time with you.

By now, you'll have realized that experiences happen all the time. By implementing experience management we can go beyond just letting things happen as they are and work to make them the best that we can. We call this a 'staged experience' since we are effectively enabling the enactment of experiences, similar to how a director might direct actors. In our case, however, we adhere to the wants and needs of the people having these experiences, using them to stage a better one for next time.

---

7    https://www.nexthink.com/press/new-research-from-nexthink-finds-employees-are-losing-two-work-weeks-a-year-to-it-downtime

Staging an experience, particularly for an organization with limited resources, can prove the benefits that adopting a stage experience can bring. One example is the Kitten Scanner by Philips: a miniature MRI scanner that uses soft toys to display the scanner's functionality to children. Children are often apprehensive about entering an actual MRI scanner, so a US-based hospital adopted the Kitten Scanner to stage the MRI scanner process with a toy cat, guiding the children through the process. This not only showed them that an MRI scanner was safe but also gave them control over the process to give them a sense of empowerment. By doing this, the hospital adhered to the wants and needs of the children – to guide them through the process in language they would understand and show them a new and scary process – in a way that was suited to their wants and understanding. They also enabled the children (effectively their customers) to be in control of the experience and provide their own input. When you adopt this approach on a bigger scale think about the experience you want to stage. What are the outcomes you want to deliver? Consider:

- Hygiene factors that are common to all

- Unique factors that only apply to you.

You do not have to be 'excellent' or 'leading' with the experience you provide, just 'good enough' for your organization. Psychology teaches us that happiness is really 'contentment' rather than 'delight'.

Consider the priority of these ambitions; how many can you manage at once? Each ambition will be a separate XLA that you will measure:

- Write your ambitions down and make them SMART:

  o **Specific**  Related to outcomes tied to both employee and business outcomes. Be direct here.

  o **Measurable**  Evaluate each ambition with experience indicators (X data, O data and T data). An ambition that is not measurable is not useful.

  o **Achievable**  They need to be ambitious (see under 'moonshot thinking' and 'psycho-logic' in Phase 4) but also achievable. This means being in the sphere of control or at least of influence.

  o **Relevant**  Related back to experience now data, business outcomes and economic factors. Experience ambitions must be relevant to the business; adhering to these factors will ensure this.

  o **Timely**  Assigned a deadline. In what timeframe should the ambition(s) be achieved? Set goals with dates: for example, a score of x within 12 months. Experience improvement projects and actions can then be created to achieve this goal.

- Begin to build your XLA stacks and visualize the connection between the ambition and supporting experience indicators.

## Phase 4 Enable

Now it is time to create the XLAs. With experience ambition/s set out, organizations now need to link relevant experience indicators (XIs) to the experience ambitions in order to enable them, and in turn the organization, to measure experience. In Enable we determine what kind of XLA is best suited to our circumstances and we understand how experience is visualized and introduced to the specific methodology that surrounds their design, so we can prepare them for implementation within the organization.

Enable begins with asking what kind of XLA you will need. For example:

- Internal IT XLA to employees
- Outsourcing company XLAs to customers' employees
- Internal companies to their outsourcers (and vice versa)
- Project XLAs.

Once you've decided, it is also recommended at this stage to understand which maturity level would be most appropriate for the XLA/s in design. We recommend level 2.0, but you can alter this depending on your resources or current exposure to the subject of experience. See section 6.4 for a full definition of the maturity levels.

Note here that whenever XLAs are put in place in an outsourcing or multi-outsourcing environment, they need to be seen as a joint commitment between the organization and the outsourcer. You can outsource experience measures, but not experience itself. All parties need to commit to delivering the same ambitions.

### The service tower problem

When we think about how to implement XLAs in the organization, we first need to address the service tower problem. Organizations appear to be structured in departmental towers. This makes sense; it is easy for us to distinguish services; the towers are not going away anytime soon. However, the issue with viewing organizations in this way is that the service tower tends to get measured in isolation, while employee/customer experience takes place across multiple towers. Therefore, if this is the case for the experience to be measured, there will likely need to be multiple XLAs, even if they are ultimately going to be focused on one persona group as in XLA maturity level 2.0.

Even if we have good SLAs, we still need something else. This is what experience comes down to. In chapter 1 we cover how service-centred surveys cannot, and are not designed to, measure the holistic experience of someone. We need sentiment surveys that adhere to XLAs to track sentiment as it ebbs and flows across the transactions of the different towers. For example, the SLA for airport parking may be separate from those for landside operations, but our experience in parking can affect our experience during the rest of our time at the airport. An early transaction can set up experience anticipation for later and it would be beneficial to people wanting to improve holistic experience to know this.

### Moonshot thinking

Occasionally, there may be no obvious solution to a concern that we find with experience, or even no solution at all. In this case, it may be beneficial to practise moonshot thinking. This is where we pick out the biggest concern that we know about within our organization. We then let go of all our mental constraints to determine ways that may satisfy those yet unmet needs surrounding the concern.

The moonshot idea originated when John F Kennedy expressed in a speech how he wanted to send a man to the moon, and is the cause of its success. That a thought so ambitious could be voiced inspires confidence. This approach has worked in various situations, such as innovations made in shopping by companies like Amazon. The final achievement is often preceded by small successes and innovations along the way. By practising moonshot thinking you may find new ways of improving experience, working or enabling experience as you strive for a seemingly impossible goal; for example, achieving a 100% happiness rate in organization-wide sentiment surveys.

However, for some experience concerns with seemingly no solution available, psycho-logic may be a worthwhile practice.

## Psycho-logic

*'It's easy to achieve massive improvements in perception at a fraction of the cost of equivalent improvements in reality.'*

**Rory Sutherland**
**Vice-Chairman, Ogilvy**

Psycho-logic means using psychology to influence experience anticipation for the better. When you apply it to a problem believed impossible or too challenging to resolve with current resources, it can be a great motivator to solving other experience concerns and provide a sense of control over the situation.

An example of psycho-logic in action is from Disney resort theme park. Customers expressed poor sentiment around queuing times for rides and attractions. They said the queue times were too long and very tedious. On the surface, this seems like a challenging concern to resolve. It was not in business interests to limit the number of customers per queue in order to ensure a very short wait as this might reduce attendance to the park. Disney solved this by altering the wait time notices at the entrance to attractions. Where the queue wait time for an attraction was advertised as 30 minutes, the actual time spent queueing would be 20. Customers were prepared for a long wait but instead entered the attraction ten minutes earlier than expected. This disproved the likely negative anticipation of a 30-minute wait and provided a positive sense of experience relief when it was perceived as being considerably shorter. So artificially inflating the advertised wait time actually made for a more positive experience.

Disney also placed entertainment within the queues for customers to enjoy. Scenery and ambience related to the ride may relieve the tedium of waiting, while actors, and recently AI, can interact with queueing customers based on their 'MagicBand' (a radio frequency device). This all combines to create a positive experience where queue times appear shorter and entertainment provides stimulation, without Disney having to sacrifice too many resources to resolve a poor experience.

Moonshot thinking and psycho-logic encourage different ways of considering how to solve an experience without conventional methods. If the experience concerns, wants and needs identified in the experience now seem unachievable, look to ways you can influence experience anticipation. It may not be possible to make an interaction more efficient but you may be able to improve the interaction within that time.

## The XLA Stack

Now that you've identified an ambition and experience indicators for your XLA, you can now set about creating your XLA Stack. XLA Stacks are already covered in chapter 7, but this is the point in the EOF where you actually create one. Organizations should create their own XLA Stack before moving onto the more technical step of building the dashboard from which they will view experience management.

## The experience reference matrix

The experience reference matrix (XRM), as well as being a section in our XLA design methodology, is also the name of the visual, dashboard view of XLAs, giving experience professionals a line of sight between the measures that comprise it. An XRM is something that is built and therefore needs to show the following related to the XLA:

- The X data

- The O data and O data scores

- The T data and T data scores.

The XRM gives the experience professional a way of interpreting the sentiment and other experience indicator data to give a conclusive statement on the state of experience. With best practices applied, surveys would ideally be distributed, along with data retrieval, and metric results from O and T data would be carried out. If this is the case, the XRM can be updated monthly, enabling a view of experience for each XLA to be seen, and how the various data points affecting the experience may be interacting with each other. By viewing this, the position of interpreting and, from there, planning experience improvement is better enabled.

The XRM is typically first built within Excel as this is a well-known tool that can be manipulated to create an effective dashboard. However, we find that the limitations of Excel can be such that organizations often then migrate the dashboard to a more powerful tool such as Power BI. Creating one first in Excel acts as the starting point to adapt to the management and utilizing of an XRM. Regardless of the tool being used, the focus of the diagram is to enable links, patterns and pathways to be observed between data points. The main links are between the sentiment (what people are feeling) and the other experience indicators (the reason behind the feeling). Figure 5 illustrates this from the perspective of experience with an IT service desk.

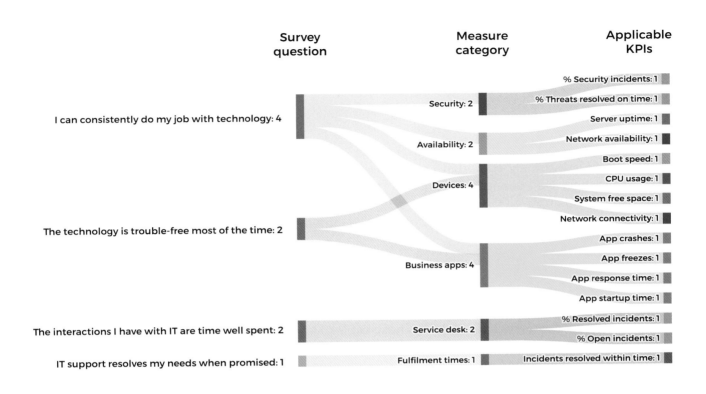

**Figure 5** Sankey diagram illustrating links between sentiment and other XIs. The diagram was created using SankeyMATIC

## The role of technology in XLAs

Technology is an indicator and enabler of experience. This does not just refer to T data; technology is an indicator in the sense that most industries rely on it to fulfil their business objectives. Aspects like availability and application crashes are an immediate technical indicator of experience and are all monitored using technology. Technology also gives us the means to measure T, O and X data through various tools. For example, ITSM tools grant us access to the relevant SLAs and KPIs for XLAs while survey tools enable us to generate and collect X data. To empower the XLA we need to align the experience indicator both with the XLA and the technology as an enabler to the XLA. X data, O data and T data are the types of technology often required as an enabler for each controllable experience indicator.

## X data technology

X data technology is the kind of technology you may be able to repurpose or already have access to. These are applications that enable surveys to be distributed, and results collected. Think of apps such as Microsoft or Google forms or more premium paid tools like HappySignals. If an X data tool is something experience professionals feel should be purchased for their organization, consider the following aspects:

- Mode of transport
- Survey design
- Sampling
- Dashboards.

## O data technology

O data tools are usually something an organization already has. These are ITSM tools, used to understand how well services have performed against their SLAs; for example, SolarWinds or Freshworks. These are enablers of XLAs as they allow organizations to see the core SLAs and KPIs that impact experience in/directly and retrieve the metric scores that act as a context behind X data.

## T data technology

T data tools, whilst not thought of as common as O data tools, are still something that many organizations use. Tools monitoring endpoint health, server health and network management tend to be commonly found. For the purposes of an XLA, Experience Collab recommends purchasing a specific digital experience (DeX) tool. These tools give insights into devices and applications but with a higher emphasis on the experience of employees using them. Examples include Nexthink, 1E, Aternity and Lakeside Software.

When it comes to finding the right technology for your organization, there are some factors to be aware of: XLA washing, extending, and bridging.

## XLA washing

This is a marketing tactic where tools, often technical tools designed to monitor endpoint, device and application health will also add an experience measurement. Whilst this can indicate interest from the tool, or the developer, in measuring experience to some degree, it can also be an effort to add a feature to the tool that will likely not provide as rich a level of detail as a tool whose main selling point is as a digital experience tool.

## Extending

The first of two more positive factors, extending is a concept where technology suppliers use sentiment data to increase the value of their core product. Essentially, sentiment data generated by the tool provider is used to inform upcoming features and updates. This is similar to washing, but with a more sincere intent. Some tools may, for example, add survey tooling to become more experience-focused after hearing it is what their customers want.

This is different from washing, where existing measures may be repurposed to give an idea of experience when the functionality of the tool actually hasn't changed. Ultimately, extending is good for the experience market as more tools observe ways of branching out into more experience-focused features.

## Bridging

Bridging is when a tool brings together experience indicators to create a better foundation for a staged experience. It is not as common as XLA washing and extending. However, some tools (e.g. Nexthink), bridge T and X data, whilst others (e.g. HappySignals) bridge O and X data. This differs from extending as the experience-focused functionality is typically an inherent component rather than something additional. This does not mean that the tool can create an XLA; that is why the XRM exists. Tools that bridge the XIs streamline part of the process of building a picture of experience for an XLA.

Bridging, in particular, is at the core of the EOF. Organizations should bridge the various experience indicators to build as contextual a picture of experience as possible so that they have full context to base any experience improvement plans on.

The Enable stage is largely focused on identifying the kind of XLA we will use for the experience project as well as the experience indicator points that we assign to each one. We have covered the three main experience indicator types and the considerations around them; for example:

- **X data**
    o   How will you understand how people feel? How will you gather sentiment?
    o   If you are going to do a survey, consider best practices.

- **O data**
    o   What SLAs and KPIs can help you understand experience?
    o   How would your existing SLAs and KPIs impact your XLA statements?
    o   Do you need more or fewer SLAs?

- **T data**
    o   What technical tools do you have that can help you gain context?
    o   Is it specifically a DeX tool? Or can it measure application uptime and health?
    o   Could this be part of your XLA Stack?

We also considered the main actions from Enable:

- Think of the type of XLA being built:
    o   Internal IT to end users?
    o   Supplier to end users?
    o   Combination?
    o   Internal IT to the Supplier?
    o   Project XLA?

- What is your experience ambition? What experience do you want to stage?
- What other data points could you gather to measure experience?
- Build your XLA Stack.
- Build your experience dashboard.

# Phase 5 Execute

The XLAs are now ready to go into operation and start measuring experience. To manage them we need to introduce a new, specialized team – the Experience Management Office (XMO). Under Execute, we introduce the XMO, the team structure, missions, scope, and roles in regard to moving experience management forward.

Experience management is a different process from traditional service management. Service management, the team which manages SLA and KPI performance, reports KPI performance periodically and is ultimately not responsible for it. In addition, the KPIs do not tend to change. Experience management, however, reports experience metrics regularly and is responsible for ensuring that experience ambitions are met. Moreover, experience can change regularly, so to ensure the factors important to customers or employees are being measured, experience indicators and ambitions themselves can change.

As well as being a different approach to service management, a dedicated XMO team will also:

- Decide the ambitions
- Agree on measures
- Calculate data scores
- Send, collect, understand, and interpret sentiment surveys, looking for patterns and pathways between data and experience
- Review O and T data measures
- Create experience improvement plans
- Action the plans
- Govern experience.

For every XMO, the mission remains the same. However, how the mission is conducted can change. There may be O and T data that is not included in an XLA, for example. XMOs will also vary in terms of size, the tasks they undertake and whereabouts they sit in the organization. Chapter 9 takes a more in-depth look at the XMO and covers the roles, scope and missions.

At the Execute stage an XMO team is required to oversee the successful implementation of XLAs in an organization. A specialized team is needed because XLAs, such as employee and customer experience, cut across multiple services and their individual towers. A specialist team that oversees the journey across them all is much more able to manage experience compared to a team within one service.

XLAs are dynamic. It may transpire that one month the experience ambition applies; the next it has been achieved. The XMO will be able to observe, by regularly collecting and analysing experience indicators, whether this is the case. Then the question arises: what other experience improvements would people like? Are the right data points currently being measured to determine this? These are all questions the XMO takes on in its role to govern experience improvement across an organization.

# Phase 6 Embrace

Phase 6, Embrace, is where we innovate the experience delivered. When experience is managed in an organization, it needs to make the most out of the results. Embrace emphasizes the importance of sharing results and action plans for improving experience. It is also concerned with experience governance, other key considerations, and how it all ties back into the experience ecosystem.

XLAs are not a one-and-done initiative. At Embrace, the XMO needs to monitor the XIs, communicate the results, and calibrate as necessary.

## *Experience governance*

The most obvious question to ask regarding experience governance is, what do our experience findings tell us? To make governance a smoother task, organizations should consider building an experience governance board (ESG). As part of the XMO leadership, a governance board can carry out tasks that include:

- Sharing business goals, outcomes and comparing them
- Identifying new experiences that need to be staged
- Sharing experience findings with complete transparency
- Identifying areas for experience improvements
- Making recommendations and/or actions for improvement
- Assessing how experience is being managed – how can it be improved?

Through governance actions, the XMO works to ensure one and/or two end-results: to improve experience and innovate the experience delivered.

## *Improve – evaluate and decide*

For the first iteration of the EOF, organizations should identify where they are. What does the experience gap show? For further iterations, where actions may have been taken, this question still applies but it also raises more. Does a gap still exist between the desired and provided experience? Remember, the lessening of the experience gap will not happen instantaneously but rather as it is measured over extended periods of time. Therefore ask these questions every time the XMO meets to analyse sentiment data.

It also needs to be determined whether a common experience is being delivered to people targeted by the XLA/s. This doesn't mean that everyone in the organization receives the same experience. Based on the XLA maturity level this may not yet be possible across multiple persona groups/departments. However, when targeting one persona group or entity within the organization, the same desired experience should be provided to them. This is known as experience parity. If one set of people from this group are not receiving the improved experience that another set are, consider why that is.

A final consideration for experience improvement: is the XRM kept up to date? If experience indicator data is being collected (sentiment, operational, and technical) on a regular basis, the XRM needs to also be kept updated on this basis. Any time where new data is retrieved but not populated into the XRM means the XMO is working with outdated, possibly now invalid data that could lead to incorrect conclusions and actions. By ensuring the XRM is populated every time new data comes in, likely month by month, the XMO is better positioned to recommend changes for the XLA and/or put plans and roadmaps into place for future experience improvement.

## Innovate

To innovate the experience desired means to act against experience dropping to its previous levels. The main concept that leads to experience dropping over time is called the gravity of average performance. This is a phenomenon where features or experience of the product/service that were once thought excellent become the new norm. As people get used to it, the performance decays from good to average as new expectations arise. As the gravity of expectations takes place, average performance will be perceived as bad. To combat this gravity, we highlight four strategies set out by Boston Consulting Group[8]:

- **Resetting mental models** In the case of experience, this refers to a reframing from service to experience. This means understanding that average performance can become bad because of how the experience has become perceived to be. Knowing this puts organizations in a better position to adopt experience improvement as a means of combatting the gravity.

- **Adopting new business metrics** For our use case, this would be the adoption of XLAs that take into account the factors leading to the gravity of expectations and working to improve them.

- **Embracing a multidimensional approach to experience strategy** Encouraging experience management across the wider experience ecosystem so that this gravity can be combatted wherever in the organization it appears.

- **Reinventing organizational capabilities** In experience management, this means using the new kind of management office, the XMO, to analyse what people want and need from their experiences to prevent them becoming perceived as average or poor.

## The changing nature of XLAs

As mentioned, XLAs are dynamic. With action plans being implemented and continual data generation and analysis, changes can occur within XLAs:

- Business outcomes

- Ambitions

- Ambition achievements

- XI question changes/rotation of questions if sampling is being used

- Metric changes (additional SLAs or new technical measures)

- Scoring/weighting edits

- Continually finding new areas to measure.

The XMO needs to continually be understanding data to learn something new about experience. This may seem like a lot of change, but it is by design. The XMO and organization need to be prepared for dynamic XLAs. This often translates to a culture/mind-shift change. While change can be a daunting prospect for organizations, it is also recognized as driving innovation. It is by

---

8    Reeves, M., Whitaker, K. and Deegan, T. (2020) Fighting the Gravity of Average Performance. Available at: https://sloanreview.mit.edu/article/fighting-the-gravity-of-average-performance/

embracing change that XLAs can be used to create more productivity and positive experiences for their employees and customers; a factor that goes on to positively affect organizational profitability and longevity. A culture of change acceptance is necessary for organizations to adopt if they want to embrace experience.

## Experience ecosystem

The experience ecosystem is a system or network of interconnecting and interacting entities, brought together to define, manage, and enhance experience. As discussed in Phase 1, the ecosystem is enabled to do the above by encouraging cooperation that cuts through service towers in an organization. There are no set limits or boundaries to the potential experience ecosystem. It will depend on ambition, scope, and ability to build coalitions of like-minded professionals. If experience improvement in one department is causing interest in another, perhaps determined through experience champions, and the resources are available as an effect of initial experience improvement, this is a way of expanding the experience ecosystem.

Note that not all ecosystems will be the same. Every organization is different; the example above won't apply to all. However, you should consider where the ecosystem is and where it could stand every time an XLA is built with personas and organizational entities in mind. Each XLA may impact different parts of the ecosystem, providing the opportunity to spread awareness of experience and experience management further. We shouldn't avoid any ecosystem potential because the success of XLAs and the XMO is proportional to the size of the ecosystem. XLAs have greater longevity when they are not confined to one entity within the experience ecosystem.

As we reach the end of the optimization framework, the main action to take away from Embrace can be summed up as maturity. Experience management is a maturity journey; start where you are with XLAs. Once you have started your journey, repeat the steps of the framework. As experience, and XLAs with them, begin to change, you can now plan where you want to be:

- **XLA 1.0** Just gathering sentiment

- **XLA 2.0** Multi-data stream XLAs

- **XLA 3.0** Applying 2.0 to personas.

Consider how you can keep moving forward and improving experience. You could engage experience champions from other entities within the organization and expand the experience ecosystem. This may lead to implementing XLAs and the framework across the organization to begin providing a better experience organization-wide.

However, before you start you need to understand whether the experience ambitions are being met. Are these working to satisfy the business outcomes? If not, look back to the XLAs. Are the right questions and experience indicators being used, or the right conclusions being drawn? If so, the next step may be to continue to improve experience where you began to realize the benefits there, or to expand the potential of XLAs to the wider ecosystem to try to provide a good experience for all.

The EOF will take you and your organization on an experience journey. We have stepped through each part of how to measure experience; however, this journey is very much an iterative one. The choice comes down to where to start and what to do once the first iteration is concluded. Keep the complete journey in mind but start where you are and focus on the next steps.

# 9 Implementing and managing experience

In the Execute phase of the EOF we introduce the XMO. It is a necessary, specialized team, not just because experience should be gathered regularly, but because it can be a volatile force. Every human is a self-programming sensor, reacting differently to experience based on past experience and prone to change.

In a group, such as a collective of employees, sentiment can alter, and quite rapidly. Humans are often influenced by group mentality. Even if someone's experience of something is indifferent, it can only take a few adverse opinions to convince them that something needs to change. Therefore, with such complexity and capacity for constant change, an XMO team is required to observe and put forward changes in XLAs and ambitions that reflect this changing sentiment. Fundamental to the XMO is answering the following two questions:

- **So what?** What does the data generated and associated with the XLA tell us?
- **What now?** What do we do and plan with the data?

## 9.1  The XMO

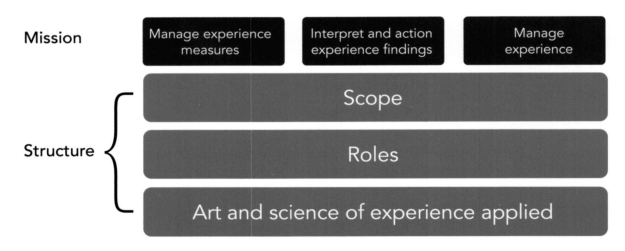

Figure 6  XMO essential architecture

The architecture of the XMO is made up of a set of missions and the structures below that support them, as shown in Figure 6. From the top down, the architecture is as follows:

- **Mission**  This is an objective that the XMO is set to fulfil as part of its overall aim to improve experience, as per the experience ambition. It has three stages:

  o **Manage experience measures**  This is concerned with the design, distribution, and collection of sentiment surveys, as well as the gathering of other experience indicator measures and populating the XRM.

  o **Interpret and action experience findings**  This means understanding what is happening and why, before determining the kind of actions that could be implemented to resolve it.

  o **Manage experience**  This refers to the task of governing and leading the XMO, setting objectives for it based on past actions or data and reporting on progress to the wider organization.

- **Structure**  The scope, roles, and art and science that are assigned to a mission. These are defined as follows:

  o **Scope**  The specific tasks that are to be carried out as part of a mission.

  o **Roles**  Positions within the XMO team that will undertake part of the scope of a mission. Some roles include designing surveys, interpreting data and XMO leader.

  o **Art and science of experience applied**  The one or more experience competencies that are assigned to a mission; e.g. the art and science of questionnaire construction and surveys that will be introduced to manage experience measures.

## 9.1.1  XMO responsibilities

The final two phases of the EOF, Execute and Embrace, are where the role of the XMO is most prominent and emphasized. The responsibilities of the XMO can be split into tasks aligned with either operational or governance, as shown in Table 1.

Table 1  XMO responsibilities: operational or governance?

| Operational | Governance |
| --- | --- |
| Interpret the staged experience | Design and maintain the outside-in and inside-out communications with the audience |
| Design/build the XLA Stack | Determine the first of two questions for the XMO: 'So what?'. What is the data telling us? |
| Create the XRM and associated dashboards | Determine the second of two questions for the XMO: 'What now?'. Suggest what to do now to meet or improve experience |
| Design and implement the experience indicators | Report on status in meeting the commitment to the defined experience |
| Implement the defined experience | Contribute to contractually valid arrangements |
| Use context to translate experience findings | Create an experience ecosystem by linking to other players of experience management |
| Calibrate experience indicators | Manage the funnel of new staged experiences |

There are seven underlying experience competencies that are typical of an XMO. These are grouped into three main themes regarding how they link to the roles of the XMO: managing sentiment, managing the measures, and managing and improving experience:

*Managing sentiment*

- **The art and science of sentiment management**

    o   How is sentiment being gathered?

- **The science of sampling**

    o   How are we ensuring a true representation of the population is included in our sentiment gathering method?

- **The science of statistics**

    o   To whom are you asking questions?

    o   How statistically valid are the responses? How able are you to get 'facts from feelings'?

*Managing the measures*
- **Data collection**

    o   Collecting O and T data

- **Scoring and weighting**

    o   How best to score and weight data points to get an accurate reflection of experience?

*Managing and improving experience*
- **The art of interpretation**

    o   How to look at experience data and draw patterns and pathways?

- **Experience leadership and governance**

    o   How to implement, manage and operate XLAs?

We will now look at each of the seven competencies grouped into their themes.

## 9.1.2  Managing sentiment

### The art and science of sentiment management

The XMO decides upon the means of gathering sentiment; e.g. by a survey or another method. Assuming a survey is chosen, they will then decide when and how to run it; e.g. through a tool or in physical form. The XMO will decide upon question techniques, design and style and how best to maximize survey responses following best practices.

### The science of sampling

Members of the XMO attempt to reduce survey fatigue by sampling: selecting a representative sample of the survey audience to receive the survey each month. This ensures that survey results are gathered for the same questions without asking the same people every month.

## The science of statistics

Here is the science where facts are worked out from sentiment. By comparing the results of surveys with the number of surveys completed versus the number sent out, the XMO can gain confidence levels set against a margin of error. As a quick overview, comparing the factors above enables the XMO to say with confidence that if the survey was repeated, the same results would occur, with the possibility of a minor deviation one way or another. With a high confidence level and low margin for error, the results of the survey truly should represent reality. For the respondents, the results are their perceptive truth.

## 9.1.3 Managing the measures

### Data collection

This competency surrounds gathering XI data. This will be sentiment as the crucial part, but also any O and T data identified as impacting experience. The member/s of the team with this role will need to understand how to obtain O data results, where T data is and how they can obtain it.

### Scoring and weighting

Once the data has been collected it needs to be weighted. This is because data points will be judged differently for each XLA. Some data points will be more important to an ambition compared to others. Sentiment is more important, in our opinion, but is T data more important than O, and by how much? The XMO decides the weighting and scoring to identify an accurate picture of experience. As mentioned in section 8.1.3, it needs to be decided exactly what 'happy' is when scoring results. This is also a task for the XMO as it will be populating the XRM with this current data so it can be interpreted for the next competency.

## 9.1.4 Managing and improving experience

### The art of interpretation

The XMO now examines the data to construct a picture of current experience. First it examines the X data to understand how people feel. Next it looks for other indicators of patterns and pathways relating to why people feel the way the X data is saying they do. By following this process, experience professionals within the XMO can understand and interpret the data. Using this interpretation the experience professionals in the XMO team can build experience improvement plans.

### Managing and governing experience

By utilizing the plans resulting from the previous stage the XMO should now be set to manage experience. This involves two things:

- Managing and improving experience
- Managing and improving how we do this improvement

To display what we're doing to improve experience and how, we need reporting. Regular reporting on data collection, interpretation and action will guide us towards the answer to two questions:

- Are we achieving our experience ambitions?
- Is experience improving?

Through reporting, we also determine whether we are working towards the original experience outcome. It also helps the XMO teams decide what to do to improve and how to broaden the experience ecosystem, thereby inviting more people into the project who might determine their own experience improvements or discuss such within their own departments.

When starting out with an XMO, there are logistical questions to ask. Is the XMO going to be a physical team, for example, or one that meets and functions remotely? The XMO lead is an essential role that should be full-time, and while the other roles should ideally be full-time, they can be part-time if needed. The XMO team will also need to decide how often to meet; for example, weekly or monthly. Monthly is the usual frequency with which sentiment surveys are distributed; however, if it is less frequent, the time of data collection and analysis should be the point when the XMO meets to review experience improvements. All such improvements should be shared and reviewed within the XMO team before being published to the wider organization.

When it comes to building an XMO, the next step is to understand the roles. Consider the following questions:

- Will the group be a specialist group or an extension of an already existing team?
- What skills are needed?

Once this is determined, to give a foundational overview, the XMO team needs to consider the following:

- Who will distribute surveys and gather sentiment? How will this be done?
- Will statistical validity be considered? Who will lead this?
- Who will match any O data and T data in your XRM and XLA Stack?
- How often will you do all of this (monthly/quarterly/other)?
- When will this be done?
- Who will populate the dashboard and ensure it is ready for a regular check-in?

From building our XMO and understanding its scope, mission, and roles to gathering and understanding the 'So what?' and the 'What now?' of our XLA dataset, communication is key. Remember, XLAs work horizontally across an organization, cutting through multiple service towers. If they are to be successful, XMO leadership will need to communicate across the experience ecosystem continuously; Figure 6 shows some of the individuals and entities who will need this information.

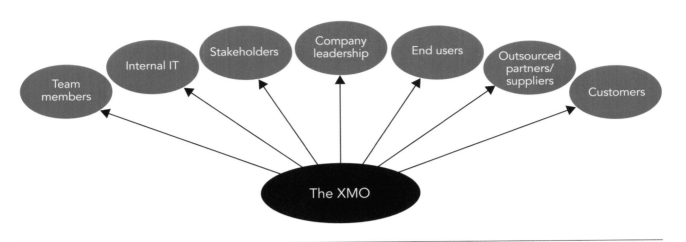

Figure 7  Who the XMO needs to communicate regularly with

Moving from left to right, XMO leadership will need to communicate to the following entities on various aspects:

- **Team members**  Team members need to understand their responsibilities; for example, survey distribution and collection, data point management, data analysis, conclusions, recommendations and governance.

- **Internal IT teams**  XMO leadership will communicate the conclusion of XMO findings or provide more detailed findings. They will recommend actions and discuss the ways in which improvement will be monitored (action planning and monitoring). This can translate to drafting new sentiment questions, monitoring further SLAs or just monitoring sentiment as IT teams take on feedback to improve their service offerings.

- **Stakeholders**  With regard to governance activities, XMO leadership will regularly need to discuss experience ambitions, successes and any failures, budget requests or recommendations and, from their findings, better ways to manage experience.

- **Organizational leadership**  As above, leadership in the XMO will need to discuss experience improvements with organizational leadership, but with a bigger emphasis on its relation to business outcomes. Using these outcomes, XMO leadership may discuss future experience ambitions based on those outcomes, discuss recommendations for experience improvement and report on successes.

- **End-users**  Using a less official tone, the XMO may need to communicate with affected end-users of the service along the lines of 'you said, we did' messaging. It may also need to build working relationships with experience champions and check in on them informally on a regular basis. Awareness of experience may need building through marketing materials and social media content, and predictions about experience improvements may need to be communicated to end-users.

- **Outsourced partners/suppliers**  The XMO will be at the centre of ensuring that the joint commitment/s between them as a customer and any service provider are upheld. It will also communicate with service providers regarding experience ambitions, any improvements for providers to potentially take up, recommendations, and action plans for any recommendations. Lastly, as the team interloping between the provider and organization, the XMO will be responsible for governing experience management in this scenario.

- **Customers**  For an XMO team within a service provider, customer experience initiatives are central to communications. This will likely relate to any experience improvements set out by the provider or requested by the customer. As a provider, reporting and the typical governance activities will be the role of the provider XMO rather than the customer as it was in the previous scenario.

Building an XMO is a commitment that shows the organization is taking experience seriously. Reporting progress towards experience improvement as an end result is the proof. Once we have XLAs ready for implementation in an organization we need an XMO team to oversee their successful implementation. We know this because XLAs, like employee and customer experience, cut across multiple service towers. A specialist team that oversees this is better equipped to manage experience than a team within one service.

We know that XLAs are dynamic. It may transpire that one month the experience ambition applies and the next it has been achieved. The XMO will be able to see whether this is the case through the regular collection and analysis of experience indicators. Then the question arises: what other experience improvements would people like? Are the right data points currently being measured to determine this? These are all questions the XMO takes on in its role to govern and maintain experience improvement across an organization.

# 10    Closing notes

Experience is universal and happening all the time in all the roles we play throughout our lives. In many of these cases, the experience provider can shape it to be the one that the stakeholder most wants. When it comes to the employees or customers of your organization you can either just let an experience happen, and risk the person perceiving it as not worth their time, or you can work to make it the kind your stakeholders are happy to spend time with and reap the benefits of doing so.

# 11   Courseware and certification

If this guide has inspired you to learn more about experience management, Experience Collab can help. We have developed a series of courses to assist organizations in understanding the importance and benefits of experience management:

- Experience Essentials
- Experience Foundation
- Experience Practitioner.

## 11.1  Experience Essentials

The starting point for all organizations new to employee experience, the experience essentials course outlines the 'what?' and 'why?' of experience and sparks that lightbulb moment. Key learning points include:

- An overview of what experience is and why it is important
- An introduction to how we can measure experience
- How to move forward with experience.

## 11.2 Experience Foundation

For those wishing to build upon the 'what?' and 'why?' of Experience Essentials, our APMG-accredited Experience Foundation course takes you on an experience journey and teaches you how to begin to build the 'how' of experience management. Through the use of experience frameworks and an XLA design methodology, the key learning points of Experience Foundation include:

- Experience strategies and ambitions
- How to measure experience
- How to govern and manage experience.

## 11.3 Experience Practitioner

The third and final course, the APMG-accredited Experience Practitioner takes attendees beyond the foundation and provides them with the practical, in-depth knowledge necessary to implement experience management in their organization. The key learning points include:

- The team, missions, and structure required to make continuous experience management a reality
- Comprehensive understanding of how to obtain, measure, and manage experience data
- Hands-on experience with the kind of tools used to manage experience.

Exams are included with the Foundation and Practitioner courses, with the opportunity to earn digital badges.